Born Again
in
America

A Nation Where Dreams Still Come True

Published by

Moraima Carballo

Port Charlotte, FL

www.bornagaininamerica.com

First Edition Paperback 2022

ISBN: 9798837720147

Design: Toelke Associates, www.toelkeassociates.com

Born Again in America

A Nation Where Dreams Still Come True

Moraima Carballo

www.bornagaininamerica.com

Dedication

*To everyone who has a dream
and the faith to pursue it.*

Acknowledgments

Thanks to my daughter, Savanna Leon Carballo, for listening to my early drafts before going to bed, and to my mother, Marina Ariste, for still being my rock. To my family and friends for letting me dream freely. Thanks to my partner, Charlie Leon. He saw me as an artist when I did not see that in myself.

Special thanks to my father, Jose Manuel Carballo who taught me to dream big.

To my editor Laurie Rosin—I had a story in my heart, and she made a book of it. She listened to my doubts and concerns and always replied with professionalism and encouragement. Thanks to the design team Toelke Associates—the cover art gave a final touch to the book.

Contents

⟨ 1 ⟩

The Dreamer

"Mija," my father would say to me, "ninety miles from here is the Land of Opportunities. Go there. Learn the language, work hard, and make me proud."

This was 2004, in Cuba, but Papa had said the same thing to me many times over the years in his endless conversations about the American Dream: If you ever have the opportunity to go to America, take it and don't look back. His favorite phrase was, "The day you put your foot on America's land is the day you are born again."

He often told me, "It is better to die in the ocean, trying to reach America, than to live here on this communist island."

I never asked Papa how he knew about the American Dream. He was not living the life he always wanted, the life he wanted for me. He blamed his failures on the communist country, Castro's regime, the economy, and the geographical location of the island.

I adored my father, and more than anything, I wanted to please him. The concept of the American Dream might be simple for Americans to grasp, but it frustrated me. I was only a child and did not understand what it meant, but with his encouragement, I felt my hope and determination grow. I decided I would achieve this dream for my father. I would make it happen, or I would die trying.

The Doorbell

My father was the dreamer; my mother was the realist. When my parents met, she was in her late thirties and had three daughters, Yamila, Xiomara, and Yuly. Mima had moved from place to place, finding work and shelter and providing for her children. At that time my father was separated from his wife, who was the mother of his young son, Manuel.

After a few months of dating, my mother was pregnant with me. Mima was not enthusiastic about adding a fourth daughter to her brood. Already she was working too hard and rarely smiled. She was in charge of the house, cleaning and cooking outside with wood because we had no kerosene for the stove. She held down a job weekdays in a candy factory while caring for us children.

It was also a sad time for her because her own mother had died the month before I was born. Before she passed away, my grandmother asked Mima to name me "Moraima."

"I almost died giving birth to you," Mima told me over and over. "I had a high fever and had lost a lot of blood. I was delirious. I opened my eyes and saw my mother in front of me, dressed all in white like an angel. She kept me alive to take care of you."

Mima is a woman of few words and a small smile. I don't remember seeing her style her hair or tend to her nails. My mother's wardrobe consisted of her work clothes and one nicer garment that she said was for a doctor's emergency or a funeral. She never had it easy. She grew up with three brothers and a younger sister, and her parents kept her home from school to help around the house.

My father was ecstatic to have his first baby girl. Papa used to sing and dance for Mima on some of his drunk days. Those were the only times I remember seeing her smile. With songs of Orlando Contreras playing in the background, he would take Mima's hand, pull her away from her cleaning, and dance with her until she joined him in song.

Papa loved his moonshine. I can close my eyes and hear him belting out thunderous melodies and my mother saying, "Manuel, the neighbors are going to hear you!" Her worse fear was that the police would come and throw him in prison because the lyrics criticized the government. Fortunately, that never happened, maybe because some of our neighbors agreed with the sentiment in Papa's lyrics and appreciated that someone was brave enough to express an honest opinion about Castro and his communist regime.

For quite some time, Papa was recognized as a great entertainer in our small community. He poured his heart out, singing melodies of regret and disappointment. On some level, he was expressing an awareness that to enjoy a happier life, either he had to change his attitude or accept that he could not change.

He was everyone's favorite. Papa was very talkative, but he was a good listener, too. When Jehovah's Witnesses came to our home to convert him, he would listen to them for hours.

"Papa, how can you listen to those people for so long?" I always asked him. He never spoke about God, and I don't think he believed in God. He believed only in the American Dream.

"I like what they talked about," he answered.

Maybe he learned to be sociable while growing up among his ten brothers and sisters. Occasionally Papa and I would drive to his parents' house in his 1957 gray-and-white Ford. I loved those weekend visits. The country air was fragrant, and mango trees towered over their front yard. Behind the house, I watched a flowing river that spoke of freedom and my eventual trip to America.

One room stored musical instruments: a red electric guitar, some drums, a piano, and maracas. "My brothers and I played music as kids," Papa told me, "and had a small group we called The Carballos."

I had the honor to see Papa singing with my uncles at a family birthday celebration, and I sang with him myself at home. As a little girl, I would sit on the concrete patio and beat out a rhythm on a cooking pan with a spoon in my right hand and a fork in the left.

I was a child when he introduced me to the bittersweet taste of moonshine. I did not understand until years later how big a problem alcohol was for him and our family.

In my memories, I was running around barefoot, giving my mother a hard time. Papa took me fishing, and he always came home with tilapia. He taught me to clean the fish inside and out, how to use a fork to rake off the scales and a sharp knife to cut off the head. I presented it proudly to Mima, and she would prepare the perfect dinner of rice, beans, and fried fish.

On occasion, Papa brought me along to his friends' house. I waited for hours while the men drank and talked about car mechanics. I was so bored that after that, I opted to wait for him in the car. "I will be right back," he would say. That promise stretched into an hour or more. Eventually he would walk unsteadily to the car, trying to hide his drunkenness. I helped Papa fall back heavily into the passenger seat. I did not know how to drive—I was much too young to qualify for a license—but I knew my way back home, and that proved to be enough.

I was his girl. He was my hero. When he was drunk, he made people laugh and feel happy. If it were not for my father, I never would have had any toys. Mima used to say she had no time to stand in line to buy toys, and only stay-at-home mothers could afford toys. Papa made toys with metal and wood, and he fashioned dolls out of empty bottles and dresses from corn husks.

My first inkling that my family had a problem started on the day that Papa bought a doorbell. I was ten years old. I opened the box and pushed the button. Ding dong! Ding dong!

"What is that?" Mima asked.

"That," my father answered, "is the doorbell we will hang on the new house I will build for you."

My mother rolled her eyes, but to me, the house was as good as built. Papa convinced Mima to move our family to a property with an old, dilapidated house behind a concrete foundation. This situation was "temporary," according to Papa.

I could see stars through the holes in the roof. During nighttime storms, raindrops on my head woke me up. I could hear Mima pushing her bedframe around her room in search of a drier spot, depending upon the wind direction.

"Just temporary," Papa would remind her.

The home had two small bedrooms and a bathroom separated by sheets of aluminum. The kitchen and living room walls had some wood in their construction. A white cloth curtain divided the kitchen from the small living room. I slept on a narrow bed in my parents' room. Two of my half-sisters shared a twin bed with metal railings in the other bedroom.

In the living room were an old black-and-white TV, a fridge, and a tiny table with four mismatched chairs. The small stove—unused because we had no fuel—sat in the kitchen, along with Mima's few pans. We used the pans to collect rainwater coming through the roof rather than to cook meals.

Papa and I walked on the foundation, and I visualized where my own bedroom would be situated. I dreamed of having a bathroom inside our new house, with a luxurious shower and a flush toilet. We would all enjoy the sound of fresh-running water clearing the drains.

"We are going to celebrate your quinceañera in this house," Papa promised as we pulled weeds growing in cracks in the concrete.

"You are still talking about building the house?" Mima asked. Her tone was harsh. She stood above us, holding a cup of coffee out to Papa. "I don't see cement blocks anywhere."

As he took the cup from her hand, he said, "This is going to be the house of your dreams, Marina!" He winked at me, and he and I laughed.

I can still picture Mama's face like it was yesterday. She was angry, but I was too young to understand why. "When you grow up," she told me, "you won't think it's funny anymore."

Sometimes when I was acting up or just being a normal child or teenager, Mima used to say, "You are just like your father." She was exasperated with Papa most of the time, and criticizing me was her outlet for bringing up his flaws. I reflected on how upset she was when he drove drunk with me in the car, but I remained loyal to my hero. He was beyond reproach.

Even at age thirteen, while ironing his clothes, I was shocked to see how short the inseam was on his pant legs. "These would fit me," I realized. How could that be possible? Papa was big and strong and very smart. Or was he…?

Was he as irresponsible as Mima said? I struggled with this and felt in the middle most of the time, torn between my love for Papa and reality as revealed by Mima. Papa spoiled me. He gave me his love and attention. He hugged and kissed me and made me believe in some crazy ideas that were just big dreams, unattainable.

A girl's *quinceañera* is a huge event, marking the passage from girlhood to womanhood. Adhering to tradition, it would be on my fifteenth birthday. If Papa said the party would be in our new house, I had to believe him. He would not subject me to a disappointment of that magnitude.

I could feel a shift within me, ever so slight but growing, where I saw my father as needing protection, and I vowed to be there when he needed me the most. I started to understand that his crazy dreams, like leaving Cuba for a new life in America, might be forever beyond his reach but might be within mine because of his positive influence.

Papa had a strong belief in the power of education. He guided me as best he could under the circumstances imposed by a communist country. From the beginning of my school years, Papa involved himself with my homework. He helped me with reading and math, and on a big wooden board he built in our backyard, he wrote out the multiplication tables in charcoal.

If he was not sleeping off a hangover, he helped Mima by getting me ready for school. She had to report to the candy factory early in the morning and never had time to brush my hair. Papa was not great at it, but he managed to skim it back into a ponytail until I was old enough to do it myself.

Once, I went to school with my uniform on backwards. When I noticed the mistake, I went to the girls' room and fixed it. By the age of five I was learning to solve my problems and take care of myself.

When I was in third grade, Papa taught me how to recite a poem with voice projection, open hands, and eloquent gestures. I got up in front of my class and began. . . .

¿Qué es el comunismo?
El comunismo es como una puerca en un corral
Que caga y vuelve a cagar
Y siempre caga lo mismo.

What is communism?
Communism is like a pig in a cage
That makes a mess and makes a mess,
So, the same thing goes on and on.

Finished, I returned to my desk. My teacher said nothing. Looking back, I understand that Papa used me to express his opinion about the communist system. In his mind, using a child to spread his condemnation would result in millions of people hearing the poem. Instead it gave the school bullies and even some teachers a pretext to make fun of me and label me "crazy like your father" for years.

Mima was furious when she heard about it. The school principal wanted to meet in private with Papa, but my father never went to the conference. His excuse was that he was working, but most of the time he came home late at night, drunk. In time, the principal just gave up.

3

The Duplex

As I entered my teens, I gravitated from my father and spent more time with my two older half-sisters, Yamila and Xiomara. Yamila was earning her degree in Veterinary Science, and Xiomara was getting her teaching degree. My eldest half-sister, Yuly, had left the house when she was eighteen to live with her father. I was too young to remember that. Since then, she had married and had two children. She visited our mother occasionally. From time to time my half-brother, Manuel, would stay with us.

We were cramped in our old home but made the best of it. Then one day Yamila announced her intention to drop out of school and move in with her boyfriend. They planned to marry. Did this mean I might have my own room at last? This was not a typical wish for a teenager in Cuba, especially in an extended family with several children. But Papa's dream of building a big new home gave me outsized dreams as well.

Papa had made no progress on constructing a home to hang the doorbell he had purchased. He blamed the economy, but Mima said the true problems were his drinking and gambling.

Xiomara came home from college with more than a bad report card; she had a positive pregnancy test. My dreams of a room of my own faded. My half-sister would move in with her baby, Andy, who would be raised not as my nephew but as my brother. Mima grimly continued cooking outside on the patio over a wood fire and working as much as she could to keep up with the bills. Some days she picked me up from school, and I stayed with her at the candy factory.

To me, it was any child's fantasy of a place to hang out. It smelled of sugar. My mother made lollipops and candy of all sizes and colors. She wore a white coat and a face mask, which reminded me of a doctor.

Papa was working, too, at a gas station. That job was perfect for him, since it allowed him to put gas in his beloved car. He was always struggling to pay for the upkeep of his Ford. He loved the freedom and status of owning a car, and he kept it in excellent mechanical condition. Working at the station also gave him opportunities to steal gas, sell it, and keep the money himself.

Moonshine was his other moneymaker, and I helped him fill two big tanks with sugar and water. While we worked, Papa continued his eternal rant against Castro and communism and his exhortations of pursuing the American Dream.

Although Papa did not make progress on our new house, he built a garage on the back of the old house. It had every tool imaginable. When I was younger, I played in the garage, although mostly I stayed on the patio because our house was so small. I shared the patio with pigs and some chickens. Juliet, our German Shepherd that Papa had found as a stray puppy in Havana, lived outside, too. No one except Andy could get close to her. When she had a litter, my little nephew was six years old, and she trusted only him to approach her or the puppies with food.

Something had changed in the atmosphere of the family. No one was humoring Papa anymore. We were dismissive whenever he brought up the idea of building a new home. No one believed him. The doorbell symbolized our miserable situation. Papa, Mima, Xiomara, Andy, and I stayed trapped inside the small box we called home, just waiting for the day to be let out.

My fifteenth birthday was approaching, and my father's promise that we would celebrate my quinceañera in our new house was a promise broken. I knew I would never see Mima make coffee on a real stove in a big kitchen. I would never hear the doorbell announce visitors.

Nonetheless, Mima and Papa worked together to make my party special as best they could. To afford my new dress, Mima worked after factory hours cleaning houses, and she collected empty bottles to return for the deposit.

For the day of "*mis quince*"—as we called it in Cuba—Papa rented our neighbors' two-story house for the celebration. My sisters came, and my close friends. Xiomara paid for a photographer, and I still have a picture of me standing on the hood of Papa's 1957 Ford, like a movie star.

A few months later, things came to a head with our living situation. Papa reluctantly sold his car, and the proceeds went to buy a different house. He refused to go with Mima and me to look at potential houses to buy.

"Your father is upset, but that old hovel is going to fall on our head one day," she said. "We need a new home!"

Mima was right, but Papa and I regretted that his dream house would never happen. The doorbell would never be affixed to a doorframe made with his hands. His Ford would never be parked in a real garage. What happened to his hopes and dreams? Papa lost them, and from the day we

My quinceañera

moved into our new house, my father seemed to be counting the days till the end of his life.

Mima and I chose a new community where all the apartments looked alike. We settled into a duplex with only two rooms and a small patio. Did Mima consider that Papa would not have enough room or privacy to make his illegal moonshine?

Papa being Papa, he always found ways to survive and ideas to raise extra money. Most were illegal, like making moonshine and stealing gasoline. His new scheme was helping people leave the country. I heard that Papa took a friend to the coast near Havana and assisted him to escape the island. He paid Papa fifty dollars in American currency. I had never seen a dollar bill until he brought his earnings home. We went on a shopping trip for shoes and clothes. That was the end of the money.

His next enterprise was to raise and sell chickens. He had seen some people buy chicks, feed them processed grain for forty-five days, then sell them on the black market. We did not have the space to raise chickens in our duplex, but Papa was not deterred. He fashioned some metal cages in my second-floor bedroom and brought in the chicks. Every morning we took the chicks from the cages, changed the water, and scrubbed the cages and the floor under them. It was a lot of work, but in forty-five days, as predicted, we had chickens to sell illegally.

The next opportunity was helping a friend on a farm that grew tomatoes, rice, and other crops. This physical labor under the hot sun drained Papa, and he was exhausted most of the time. He looked older by the day. Still, he hustled to make extra money in a terrible economy so our family could survive.

I noticed he cut back on his moonshine consumption. Occasionally he would have a drink at home with one of his brothers. Otherwise, he was trying to put food on the table and help Mima pay the bills.

I did not want to leave my parents while they were enduring difficult times, but I had no choice. We lived in a small community with no secondary school, and my parents had to decide where to send me to earn my high school diploma. One option was a boarding school, but Papa thought I might come back pregnant or drop out without the influence of a watchful guardian. They settled on my living with one of my father's relatives.

In retrospect, being separated from my parents in my teen years helped me build character. I learned to be more independent and watch out for myself.

I lived with my father's cousin Monday through Friday and went home on weekends to see my parents. Traveling from the city into the country was a challenge.

On one visit, Yamila and her boyfriend were at our apartment, drinking. Her boyfriend had built a horse-drawn carriage, and he drove me back to the city in that on Sunday night. I felt like a star in a Western. It was terrifying and exciting. Yamila and her boyfriend were singing and drinking, and the horse was going faster and faster down the middle of the street. Was the horse drunk, too? I never thought we would arrive alive.

Every weekend, until I graduated, I used a different type of transportation—whatever I could find—including carriages, bicycles, and occasionally a bus.

As soon as I earned my diploma and moved back home, Mima issued an ultimatum: "Find a job or continue your schooling. I don't want you hanging around in the house."

I understood where she was coming from. Cuban women without a job or education were in a bind. She drew from her own experience—single, with daughters from three different fathers. People had many names for women like this. I respected my mother for never letting her upbringing and hardships stop her from being a good mother. By that I mean "provider." She never learned to be affectionate. For her, kisses and cuddles were a waste of time.

My employment options were few in our small town. A tobacco factory was near our house, and I could marry a country man, have a few children, and live happily ever after.

That would be easy.

The other option was to leave home again and attend college. With better luck than my sisters, I would come back with a diploma in my hands.

I might have gone that route, but one night I went dancing at a club and met a local boy with a sweet cowboy smile. From our first salsa, Rodolfo and I were as much in synch as professional dancers. We laughed and sang together, and from that night we were inseparable.

Our time together was very romantic. Every night the sky was filled with stars. The stars were happy for us. They were so bright, they sparkled. The sky spoke to me of love. Liquor was illegal, but love was free. Most of the time we were dancing and drinking. Sometimes we played dominoes. I was happy.

At eighteen, we married in a small, picture-perfect wedding with music, friends, and family. I wore a long, beautiful white gown and carried a bouquet of roses. Confidence and pride shone from my blue eyes. I was only four feet, nine inches, but that night I felt tall, elegant, and very special, like every bride, as my parents stood by my side.

Rodolfo and I went on a three-day honeymoon to a small hotel, Cuba's Rainbow, in the area of Soroa. Its natural beauty was enchanting and captivated my heart.

We settled in at my parents' apartment. I worked at the tobacco factory. My husband did not have a job. One Sunday morning, I found him in our bedroom, throwing T-shirts and pants and the rest of his belongings into his green backpack.

"Are you leaving me?" I asked. I couldn't believe it.

He kept his head down, ignoring me.

"Why are you leaving me?" I asked.

He needed a few minutes to answer. He took a deep breath and replied, "Your mother does not want me here any longer."

Silence weighed down the room.

"I will not stop drinking," he continued by way of explanation. "This is who I am. When you met me, I was a drinker. My drinking should not surprise anyone."

He flung his backpack over his shoulder and brushed past me without another word, not even "goodbye."

He did not have many things to pack, but after he was gone, the room felt empty, as if he had taken everything. I got into bed and stayed there, crying with the pain of a broken heart. For days I was lost and confused. I thought it was the end of my life, even though being a divorced teenager was common among the many, many uneducated country girls in my town.

In my mind I replayed our last moments together. I should have done more to stop him, I thought. But he never said, "Come with me."

I was furious with myself, and I was livid with my mother. Most of all, I was enraged that Rodolfo had chosen a bottle of rum over me and our love. "Not even good rum," I fumed, "like Havana Club. No, he replaced me with moonshine, rotgut!"

For days Mima came to my room to talk to me, but I turned away from her, refusing to speak. Maybe she had done the right thing—like when she pushed Papa to sell his car and buy a new home—but I hurt too much to think rationally.

How could she do this to me? Hypocrite! My husband was just like Papa, whose best qualities were his dancing and drinking. Mima stayed with Papa, and they danced and sang and drank moonshine. She was happy . . . sometimes. So why wouldn't she allow me to follow her example? I challenged her on this point, but she did not agree with my reasoning.

I felt humiliated. In our small community, everyone knew everyone else's business. They thought they knew what was best for me and did not hold back their opinions.

"You were too young!"

"Good thing you didn't have children!"

"Don't worry, Morey. He will be back soon."

That was my favorite comment. It gave me hope.

Deep in my heart, though, I knew Rodolfo had left for forever. He had chosen his own way to freedom, as much as I was not able to under-stand it.

After a few weeks, I saw him in clubs, and his drinking was out of control. He got into brawls. He had no job. He found another girlfriend. The next year, they had a baby.

4

The Green Scarf

I was still working at the tobacco company, reporting to work between six and seven AM, when the factory doors opened. The strong smell of tobacco woke up anyone who was still sleepy. All of us women started our day by grabbing a huge, empty sack and filling it with tobacco leaves that had been harvested. Tobacco technicians weighed each bag we were responsible for, and our overall goal was to classify all the leaves in the bag and strip them from the stem and center vein without damage, and then smooth them out, arranged with other leaves in the same classification.

All this was done in stages. First we dragged the packed bags next to identical chairs and small tables organized in rows, like a classroom. Working with our hands as quickly as we could, we began the process of stripping the leaf from the stem. To keep our job, we had to categorize every leaf in our bag into a specific grade within eight hours.

It was not easy. Some days were more difficult than others. Often, I thought I would never finish, especially when I was a new employee. I would look inside my bag to check my progress, and it appeared that more leaves have been added by a cruel trickster.

To sort each leaf into a specific grade, I took them one by one from my sack, "ironed" it by hand, and arranged each one by size, color, and imperfections. Also considered were the smell, color, texture, and complexity of the small veins on each leaf. I meticulously stripped each leaf from its central vein. Any leaves that had not been damaged by the sun or chemicals or torn would be deemed the best. These would have a specific use as the final touch, the outer wrapper of the cigar. Medium and small leaves had their own purpose, no matter how damaged. Nothing was wasted.

One older woman knew each leaf like a mother knows her child. She and others like her made sure that we new workers understood the characteristics of each leaf while working with it. In my first days, I accidentally damaged some of the leaves while stripping them. The old woman in the chair next to mine looked over the rim of her eyeglasses like an elderly schoolteacher. She explained that with passion and discipline, I would learn to strip each leaf and protect it.

The sorted leaves were baled and transported to the city of Havana, where they would mature in storage for a very long time . . . or so I heard. I had never seen that for myself. That done, other workers in factories specifically for the purpose would produce the magical Cuban cigar that is still considered the best in the world.

My memories of those days have not faded. I can still smell the tobacco and hear the ladies' loud laughter and singing. At eleven o'clock every morning, the factory became as quiet as a ghost town, and for forty-five minutes we listened to a popular radio drama as we worked. When the program ended, some of the women began to argue, having opposing opinions about the characters, their behavior and decisions, and the direction of the plot. The conflict was never serious, and soon everyone was laughing and smiling again. It was a good environment for someone as unhappy and depressed as I was after my husband left me.

Papa rolled his own cigars, wrapping them inside a big, good leaf and cutting the edges with his own hands. He would admire it, appreciating his small work of art. He put the cigar in his mouth and lit the end, relishing the raw, natural fragrance. This was the only little freedom that he still had. Moonshine was illegal; expressing his opinion about Castro was condemned, and prosperity was beyond his reach. But Cuban tobacco was still accessible to him. He lay on the sofa, watching the same depressing news, while smoking a natural Cuban cigar. Sometimes he fell asleep and dropped the lit cigar on the rug. I would rush over and pick it up. It was a nightly ritual.

After a time, a new woman came to work in the factory. We were the youngest employees and became friends. Anita and I were a good influence on each other, not wanting to end up like our much-older coworkers who had spent decades sorting tobacco leaves. Like me, Anita was a high-school graduate, so we both qualified for a new program she had heard about, to earn certification as aides to computer teachers. We would be professionals.

I applied to the program and was accepted. I was very excited to be around computers for the first time. In 2001, every school in Cuba had the opportunity to create its own computer lab, so job opportunities would be abundant. We would be on the leading edge of a fantastic new field.

It wouldn't be easy, though. Transportation was—and still is—very difficult on the island, and the classes were far from my small town.

Anita and I persevered. I sat at my monitor and learned the ins-and-outs of Microsoft Word®, PowerPoint®, and Excel®, among other educational, interactive software. We did not, however, have access to the

Internet. I didn't miss what I never had. Just learning the new world of technology was for me, Anita, and our schoolmates like discovering a whole universe. It changed my life.

The school where I would work was relatively close to my small town. As the computer teacher, I was known as "La Maestra de Computation." Apparently people forgot that not too long before, I was a girl in the tobacco factory. That identity faded from me.

Mima was delighted for me. When I brought Papa to the computer lab, his eyes shone with pride and wonder. From his expression, I knew he was marveling at how ahead I was of my time. He saw a different future for me, on top of the world. In many ways he was right.

His own future was bleak, and in retrospect, I knew his past had been no better. I found this unsettling, confusing. To me, Papa was the smartest and strongest man on earth, so how could he have allowed his misery and alcohol to immobilize him? He railed against the communist system but never escaped the country, even though he had opportunities to do so. One day I asked him.

"Papa, in 1980 when Castro opened the port of Mariel in Havana, and when you arranged a boat for a friend, why didn't you leave?"

"This is the land of my birth, and I grew up here," he replied. "The air is fragrant with cigars and sugar cane. If anyone should leave, it should be Castro and his followers."

My father's pride deprived him of seeing a new horizon . . . or even seeing what was in front of him. He never found what was on the other side, nor did he learn how to live on this side.

I had a revelation. Seeing how stuck he was, I felt motivated to leave the country and see the world. I had proved to myself that I had the power to better my life. I struggled, though. I had no idea how to put my goal into action.

My friend Anita told me she was completing an application she had picked up at the American embassy in Havana. The purpose was to obtain the status of political refugee for her family. Intrigued, I accompanied her to the embassy several times.

Suddenly America seemed within my grasp. I could live the American Dream and have a big house like the one Papa promised to build. I could drive an American car like the one Papa sold so we could afford a better place to live. And I would bring Papa with me. When we arrived, I would tell him, "Look, Papa! This is freedom. We have the liberty you

My last birthday with Papa

always told me about. We are in the Land of Opportunity!"

Anita and I used to ride bicycles together almost every day after work. We met in the middle of the road and hung out for a while. The heat rising from the asphalt felt like flames engulfing us, but she and I talked for hours. I wish I had photographs from those days, but this was before the ease of cell-phone cameras or social media that demanded selfies.

My birthday is July 3, and hers is July 4, one year apart. On our last birthday together, we celebrated at my house. One month later, she and her family were ready to leave for the United States. I stayed at her house overnight. We cried and laughed and finally said goodbye.

For quite some time, my days returned to normal. My friend sent photographs of herself in America. Their colors were like a rainbow after a stormy day. I could smell her happiness and freedom. The glossy prints reminded me of the crystal water on the river behind my grandmother's house.

I shared the pictures with my boyfriend and Papa. When my father looked at them, I saw melancholy in his eyes and heard sorrow in his voice. I can envision him now, standing next to the kitchen table, saying his favorite phrase, "Your friend has been born again in America."

Did he realize that after many years, nothing had changed, and new generations were abandoning the island? Did they have more courage or confidence in the uncertainty of the future than he had? He had put his trust in moonshine and his ideas than in his ability to build a new future. New generations were embracing the unknown and exploring the possibilities in front of them in Cuba. Papa might have felt sorry for himself for not taking the risk of leaving the island or learning how to work within the system.

Instead he hoped for freedom or a different economy or more unity or perhaps less division—whatever it would take for his magical thinking to become reality. At one point Papa was collecting signatures on a petition that supported democracy. He and many others had collected ten thousand signatures.

Papa had been inspired by President Jimmy Carter, who visited the island and met with Fidel Castro in 2011. The president lifted all travel restrictions from the US to Cuba.

My father was arrested for gathering signatures and taken to the police station, where he received a warning not to repeat such behavior.

His arrest taught him that democratic society or government could not, would not, happen at home. He was no longer young and had not seen what was on the other side. I don't know if the police had threatened him or just given him a citation for circulating the petition. I know only that five months later, he was dead.

I was at work when I found out. The students and teachers sang the national anthem at nine AM and went to their classrooms. I was in the computer lab with my group when I noticed a student hovering just outside the door. I went over to him, and he said, "Maestra, tu Papa se murio."

Teacher, your father has died.

I was in shock. I stared at the young man, not knowing what to do. Then I gathered my belongings and began to run from the school to my house, which was two miles away. As I approached, I recognized a group of neighbors gathered in front of our house. I fell into emotional turmoil. I was angry they were there, like spectators at some performance. Then fear overcame me. I did not want to enter the house. I did not want to see my father and find the indisputable truth.

I forced myself inside. Papa was lying on the couch, like every night, when he smoked a cigar and watched the news loop again and again until he fell asleep. Many times I had picked up the tobacco scattered on the floor after he dozed off.

This time, something was different. I was terrified. I looked down at him. He was dead. I sank to the floor next to the couch and lay down next to my father's body. His jaw was slack but hardening. I held his jaw and closed his mouth, then secured it with a green scarf I had with me. I cried and cried until no more tears came from my eyes or my heart or any other place that hurt so much. I felt weak, cold, and numb.

For a moment I thought Anita was standing in front of me. My grief was so intense, I was hallucinating. I needed her to be with me, so my addled brain conjured her image.

Mima and I clung to each other and sobbed. "Do not leave us," I cried.

Never again would we sing together and drink that moonshine that kept us alive or killed us slowly.

Two hours later, the ambulance arrived. The men transported Papa's body to the hospital for the autopsy. Then he would be taken to the only funeral home in the city—we did not have one in our rural area. The funeral home brought Papa to our house in a coffin. The autopsy found that he had died of a heart attack.

Alone, I closed myself in my bedroom and argued with God. I had always been a believer in my own way. I had faith that something extraordinary was with me. On my bureau was a small, plaster statue of San Lazarus, one of the saints most Cubans believed in. I used to call San Lazarus "God."

When I was in my teens, my half-sister Yuly was dealing with a diffi-cult pregnancy. Mima was worried Yuly would lose the baby or her own life. I had gone to my bedroom and cradled the statue in my hands. I prayed to him and promised that if he took care of my big sister and her newborn, I would travel to Havana, to the Sanctuary of San Lazarus, and donate $20.00 in pesos cubanos to his plate.

He answered my prayers, and I fulfilled my promise.

Now I talked to him again. I thought God could not take my father from me. I was only twenty-two! I needed Papa for life advice. "Why did you take my father?" I demanded. Being so young, I did not compre-hend death, nor life, nor anything else at that point. I was not equipped to understand the loss of my father. I was not ready to lose the person who meant everything to me. The grief I felt when my friend left for America was different. I was grief stricken but happy for her.

Guilt assailed me. I thought of the times I had borrowed money from Papa and promised to pay him back but never did. If I had another chance, I would pay him back every peso and shave his face and work on the farm if that was necessary. If I had the chance, I would tell him that the promises of a new home did not matter to me, and neither did the promise to take me to the José Marti museum.

For one night we watched over my father's body at home. Friends and family gathered to share our grief. Everyone felt sad for us. Even my ex-husband came to pay his respects. I was annoyed, feeling Rodolfo had intruded, but Mima pointed out that he had remarried and had a family and was happy with his new life.

We buried Papa, and the house felt empty without him. That feeling was permanent. Many nights I went to bed crying. I slept with Mima and buried my face in my father's pillow, which still held his essence.

The night before Papa died, we had been sitting on the front porch of the house, and I remarked on how sad he looked, and how disheveled.

"Papa, why haven't you shaved?"

He looked at me but did not answer.

"I will buy you a new razor blade tomorrow," I told him.

His eyes held unfathomable sadness. "I am tired, not just physically but mentally."

His last message to me was, "Sometimes we just want to die because we have been dead for a while."

Neither he nor the system nor the economy had changed since Castro took power.

Now I accepted that Papa did not want to live anymore. The disappointments kept mounting up, and he had stopped trying. He did not have the heart for it. If only I had detected the despair, I could have talked to his heart and not let him go.

Papa's life was over, but I knew for certain that his soul would be in America. If I fulfilled his dream, I would be close to him again.

While I was advanced in my career beyond most people in Cuba, compared with other countries all over the world, I was years behind in my computer skills.

I worked Monday through Friday in the lab, and every Saturday I took continuing education classes in Computer Science. I did this for myself, my future, and my father.

‹ 5 ›

Foreteller

I did not want to live in that small town anymore. Lonely and angry, I needed to move from that place where my father had suffered so much failure and regret. My boyfriend helped me find a second-floor apartment in a city not far from my hometown. I managed to persuade Mima to come with me, to leave behind her sad memories of sharing a life with Papa in that duplex.

In my favor was that Yamila lived near our new apartment, and she had twins. Mima stayed busy and happy by helping with her grandchildren. I, meanwhile, continued to work as a computer teacher, assigned to another school nearer our new home than my previous one.

I was meeting new friends, including our upstairs neighbors. Our small-talk deepened into conversations, and I discovered that this couple and I had much in common. They, too, harbored a crazy dream of making a new life in America. We did not like the system, and the system did not like us.

We agreed to leave Cuba at the risk of our lives. While they talked about a "better life," I set my sights on a "new life." Like Papa said, "Be born again in America." I did not want to go to the United States and have any of the same conversations I was having now on the island. I did not want to sound nostalgic for any so-called good old days. I wanted to

29

be reborn as an American, as Papa had taught me: speak English, travel in my new country, and find mountains to inspire the same awe in me as the extraordinary Pinar Del Rio. I added to those intentions. I would leave behind bitterness, hatred, racism, and resentment. I would never allow myself to blame something or someone else or the system when things went wrong.

My objective was to create the ideal life that eluded my father. Papa died without knowing freedom or learning to exist within a communist system. I vowed that would not happen to me.

For me, it was also too late to learn how communism works. In my state of mind, everything about this country was too late.

I learned about the Cuban revolution in school and by listening to Papa's lessons at home. My history professor's version was at odds with Papa's, leaving me confused. Which version was reality? My professor regaled his students with stories about how many brave souls sacrificed their life for the revolution, with Castro himself in the front lines. This brave leader was not the man Papa had described.

School also taught me from a young age that Camilo Cienfuegos, one of Castro's top guerilla commanders and appointed head of the armed forces, died under suspicious circumstances in a small Cessna over the Straits of Florida. The plane and his body were never found, and Cienfuegos immediately became a martyr.

Papa taught me that Castro had Cienfuegos murdered because the commander did not agree with his ideas. "Those who did not live by Castro's doctrines disappear," my father said.

"I must leave Cuba and find the freedom and dreams that Papa never found here," I told myself. Did I want the American Dream or simply a new horizon, far from the same negative conversations I had been hearing my whole life, which cast a gray and black pall over everything.

Misery prevents people from seeing the true colors of Cuba, a tropical paradise with vibrant colors muted by the overlay of gray and black. They were people like my father, who could not see even the most stunning rainbow because their thoughts and attitudes painted their whole existence with gray and black.

Ironically, the people who managed to escape would miss all they had left behind, even the gray and the black.

The first step for putting my plan in motion was to visit a woman who predicted the future through Santeria, a fusion of Catholic and African folk beliefs. It emerged in Cuba in the 1600s and been a part of our culture since then. In fact, Santeros outnumber Catholics by eight-to-one. The island is the religious center for the practice, but it has spread to many countries. Seeking her guidance about my future was not far-fetched in my society.

I had consulted her before, about other issues, and I trusted her. I parked my bicycle and entered her house. The big Black woman recognized me with a wide smile. She wore white voluminous clothing, and a white ribbon tamed her hair. I hoped for some mystical reinforcement to keep me believing in my dreams.

She had arranged statues of her saints on the floor in the corner of the front room, amid flowers and offerings of food to the deities.

She gestured me to one of two chairs facing each other at a small table. The smell of tobacco, rum, and heavy perfume enveloped me.

"You are planning a trip in the water," she began.

That did not prove anything; half the population of Cuba was looking to leave the island by water or airplane for a simple change of scene.

"This is dangerous," she continued. "You could die in the choppy water."

I felt as if she had punched me in the stomach. This was not what I wanted to hear! I did not want to drown.

"You have a bright future here in Cuba," she concluded.

Some minutes in silence told me she was finished. I paid her ten pesos Cubanos and left. "She must be right," I thought. Only she can see into the future. To me it was an unknown. Besides, that trip on the water was dangerous. I could die.

My father's words since my childhood warred with the fortuneteller's. I heard him say, "If you ever have the chance to leave, do it and never look back. It is better to die in the middle of the ocean, trying to leave this communist country and find liberty and great opportunities, than to die here, while you are still alive."

I had wasted those ten pesos Cubano, I decided. Why did I spend money on something I already knew and had been clear to me? Was I waiting for her to soothe me with "You don't have to leave to find freedom. You can learn to mix gray and black and make a rainbow. If you numb your pain with moonshine, you can learn to live under a dictatorial system with pride and confidence."

That woman did not understand what I was craving. I was yearning for hope.

⟨ **6** ⟩

Sugar Cane

Papa was right about the importance of freedom of speech and how it had been quashed in Cuba. When I was working as a teacher, I learned to keep my mouth shut and keep my beliefs to myself. If I ever risked even a veiled conversation that hinted against Castro or the system, someone would call me aside and urge me to be more circumspect.

Once, one of my superiors decided to talk to me about capitalism. We left the school grounds and sat on a bench in a public park. He explained how capitalism works. The man was eloquent and authoritative as he expressed his point of view.

"People die on the street in America for not having medical assistance," he said. "Homeless people are everywhere, unable to pay rent. They, too, are dying by the thousands."

I was only twenty-four, but I would not let him brainwash me with the old arguments about how privileged we Cubans were with access to free education and free health care. He had not accomplished his objective of changing my mind when we walked back to campus. By this time, I had friends and family living in America, and they were happy.

My new friend Sonia invited me to her birthday party, where I met her boyfriend, Alien, and her sister, Dian, and her ten-year-old nephew. They had more influence on me than my school administrator. After getting to know one another, we started talking about leaving the island. The music was loud, and it muffled our conversation. They said anyone wanting to leave would each need to pay the boat owner $10,000 for gas, water, food, and taking the risk. My heart sank. I did not have that kind of money, nor did any family nor friends to lend me that amount. My dreams were dashed.

As the festivities wound down, I left the party with my new friends. On the way home, we continued to discuss leaving Cuba, and I said I could not accompany them because of the finances.

"My family might help us," Alien said.

His words ignited my hope, but at my core, I felt we were just dreaming. We kept walking and laughing and planning what we would do in Miami.

That hope faded as months passed. I settled into a routine. I bicycled to work early in the morning and came home to Mima in the late afternoon. I sat down at the kitchen table with a hunk of Cuban bread, oil, salt, and garlic and tell my mother about the day's work.

Early one morning, I heard pounding at my front door. Sonia brushed by me when I let her inside. She looked agitated and burst into tears.

"My husband left Cuba," she sobbed. "I am so afraid for him!"

"When will you get some news?" I asked.

"Not until he can send me an email that he made it to the States."

She was inconsolable, and nothing I could say would help. The voyage was dangerous, and I remembered the fortuneteller's warning to me. Sonia had to keep herself controlled so as not to raise suspicions, and we could not confide in anyone because we could be arrested for being aware of an illegal departure.

I learned more about my friend during this time. Her parents had died when she was nine and her sister, sixteen. Sonia shared stories about how difficult their lives had been. She was no stranger to adversity, and now she feared losing her husband. She cried thinking of him, and she desperately wanted to leave the country.

At last Alien got word to Sonia. He was safe but not in Miami with his family. He had landed in Mexico. At that time, that was the only way he could get into the States, but it would not happen for months.

Finally he was reunited with his family, and they helped him get settled. Now that Sonia knew Alien was safe, she was on fire to reunite with him. Her strong desire to escape reignited the hope in my heart. Salvation was a mere ninety miles from Cuba.

"When your plans are in place," I told her, "don't forget about me here. You go first, then I will follow."

Going through this ordeal together, Sonia told me more about her own family. Her older sister, Dian, was divorced, living on her own, supporting her son. She, too, hoped for a better future for herself and her boy.

Not long after, I stood on my balcony on a rainy day and looked down at children sloshing around in the flooded streets. Sonia came into my line of vision on her bicycle, her hair flattened by the showers and plumes of water sent up in the wake of her bicycle tires. I went to my front door, and my friend stood there, holding her bicycle.

"Do you want to come with me to Miami tonight?" she asked. Her eyes were as clear as the droplets falling from the sky.

"What are you talking about?" I asked, confused.

"I know a man who said that in two days, a boat from Miami is coming to the Los Palacio coast to pick up a family. He has room for more passengers."

I stared at her, my heart pumping hard.

"My husband will help you as soon as he finds out that you are coming with me on the boat."

We stared at each other. We were both afraid, but we both wanted to leave Cuba. This would be my first attempt to escape, and the idea was electrifying. I agreed to go. Now there would be no changing my mind. Leaving that night, within a few hours, left me almost no time to think.

I went to tell my mother. She was the only one I could trust with my plans, and I swore her to secrecy. Her eyes were full of worry. If anyone found out, we could be thrown in jail. I packed a light jacket, blue jeans, tennis shoes, and a blouse and tied my hair up into a ponytail. Then I kissed my mother goodbye, hating that I had to leave her alone. We agreed that if I did not come back to our apartment after two days, she would go to Yamila's house and tell her I was gone. Until then, Mima was sworn to secrecy. We lived in an apartment building where everyone knew everyone else's business.

My friend and I strolled along the street like any two friends. We were on our way to meet the man charged with guiding us to the boat. It was a thirty-minute walk to his house and a two-hour drive to Los Palacios.

Inside the Jeep, we did not introduce ourselves to the other passengers or try to make small-talk. Sonia and I huddled in the backseat, not uttering a word.

The men in the front seat spoke in low voices . . . very uncharacteristic of Cubans, who talk rapidly in a high pitch. Their conversation only emphasized the danger.

When we reached our destination, Sonia, her friend, and I climbed out of the car without a word to the driver. We walked away as quickly as we could. I had no idea where we were heading. Ahead were sugar cane—tall, study grasses with sharp edges that towered over us. I heard voices ahead, and a flashlight shone its beam at us. I was terrified.

Strangers joined us, and we fought our way through the cane. It cut into my hands and face.

Sonia reached to hold my hand tightly, but again and again we tripped on the detritus and jagged, severed stalks left behind from previous harvests. Many times we stumbled and fell but helped each other to our feet. It was a nightmarish odyssey through the plantation fields. We were drenched and hungry and exhausted but had no choice but to keep going.

Sonia and I were the only women. The rest were men, and some came prepared with machetes and knives. I worried because some were drinking on this dangerous trek. Finally we reached a small canal, which we had to cross, holding our cell phones and backpacks overhead. The water was cold, and it stank. Quietly, following the leader, we climbed out of the canal and walked in single file toward the coast. First we had to slog through a mangrove swamp. I was drained of energy. The mud sucked at my feet, and I was afraid I would lose my shoes when I struggled to free myself. Every step was agony.

I could sense the closeness of the ocean. The air had a different quality than the cane fields. When I could hear the waves, I was elated. Now we would wait for the boat.

Good sense told me to keep my distance from the men, but I was so hungry and weak, I risked approaching them and asking for something to eat. Someone had bread and black sugar. I asked for a piece of bread, and he tore off a bit and gave it to me. I went to share it with Sonia. I found her sobbing.

"What is wrong?" I asked.

In my brief absence, the organizer of our escape, who was leading our trek, called Sonia's husband in Miami. Alien said she and I would have to go back home. He would not allow us leave with this group of men.

"Why not?" I asked in disbelief.

Sonia explained, "The boat that will pick us up will head to Mexico, taking a route where the Cuban Coast Guard is less likely to spot us. Alien says it is not safe for two women alone, without a man to protect them, in Mexico, waiting to cross the border into the US."

"But—" My heart sank, and my hopes were dashed. After all the effort we had put into this night, the last thing I wanted to do was throw it away or do this all over again at another time.

"He screamed at me," Aida continued, "because his fear for us is so strong. He said we must both go back home."

I took a moment to reconsider. "That is fine with me," I told her. "I came with you, and I will leave with you." After all, I myself was afraid of these armed strangers who were drinking, although I would never say that to her.

My feet hurt, my arms were bruised and cut, and so were my legs. I stank from the canal. I knew that time and sleep would heal my body, and a hot shower at home would take care of the stench. "Vamonos! Let's go," I said, resigned.

We announced to the other travelers that we were going back home. An older man—maybe in his late fifties—said he would join us. He, too, was afraid of going on the boat.

At sunrise we walked out of the mangroves. With good fortune sending us on a different route, we did not have to cross canals or fight our way through the sharp grasses. We were walking on a pebble road. The plantation was to our right and left.

A man on a bicycle passed us. We asked if we were near the main road, and he replied it was a few hours ahead by foot. We kept walking until dusk and at last came upon a town. There, a tractor was about to leave with some farmworkers, and the driver allowed us to climb on. He took us to the next town, and then we were on the highway to San Cristobal, where we lived.

Between catching rides with the tractor and Jeeps that stopped for us, we finally made it to my doorstep. It was very late at night. I knocked on the door, and Mima opened it.

I saw that my mother had been crying and now was overjoyed to see me. She pulled me to her and then hugged Aida. She fed us hot soup, and then I said goodbye to my friend and took a shower to wash off the dirt and dried blood and canal smell.

I fell into bed. When I awoke comfy and warm but aching in my own bed the next morning, I decided being in Cuba was not all that bad after our terrifying night. I decided to forget about America.

I stayed home from work to recuperate. My feet had blisters from the mud pulling at my shoes, and my legs were on fire. My thighs were raw from my denim jeans chafing against my skin. For days I wore sandals, but that was the only clue something unusual had happened. No one noticed.

Better To Die on the Ocean

I gave up my dreams, but Sonia had other considerations—her husband was in Miami, and she held the hope that they would be reunited someday soon.

Because so much of our bond was based in our desire to escape the island, our friendship eventually faded. I went back to my job, and she continued her own life. In time, with better luck, her husband managed to get her out of Cuba and into the United States. Rather than being invited to join her, I was not even aware that she had left. I found out from her sister, Dian, and her son at their apartment.

Soon I felt that I had more friends in Florida than in Cuba. My desire to join them reignited. I reestablished contact with Sonia. I used my cell phone to call, and she called me and sent emails. Occasionally she sent photographs to her sister and me. I recall one particular picture in which she was wearing a black dress and high heels. She looked amazing.

One day I received a call from Sonia. "I have some connections for a boat that is coming to America," she said. She wanted me to take that trip and help Dian with her ten-year-old son.

I was surprised and frightened. For once, I did not have money. What would happen if I got to America, and they asked me to pay them?

I decided my father and San Lazarus would take care of me and make the trip possible.

I had to confide in Mima. She was also nervous, but we both decided to trust and have faith in the midst of uncertainty.

Unlike my previous attempt to leave, I went to Yamila's house with Mima the night before. I told her and her husband, Luis, of my plans as we had a cup of coffee. Luis, who was soft-spoken and polite, surprised me with his encouragement. He told me to take a risk and leave. Yamila, on the other hand, was angry and disappointed. Perhaps she was remembering when she wanted to leave Cuba but was too afraid to take the chance. Deep in her eyes, under her disapproval, I saw hope. She told me what I had said to Sonia months before: "Don't forget about us here."

I hugged my sister hard, then kissed Luis and their eight-year-old twins. I did not know if I would ever see them again.

Finally the day of departure arrived. Mima and I left our house in San Cristobal early in the morning. I was to meet Dian and her boy in front of the hospital, which was a twenty-minute walk from my house. Mima and I did not say a word to each other. Because the area of the public hospital was always busy with pedestrian traffic, we felt no one would notice Dian and me and the child getting into the car that Dian had arranged to take us to Havana City.

As we approached my destination, I stopped under a shade tree and turned to my mother. "I have to go on my own from this point," I told her, and kissed her goodbye. My heart was breaking into pieces. First I had lost Papa six years before. Now I was leaving my mother, just to find my own fortune. For a moment I considered giving up on my dream or trusting what the fortuneteller had told me. On some level, I hoped

Mima would ask me not to go. If she had, I would have walked with her back home.

But she didn't, even though her blue eyes brimmed with tears. She was well aware of my father's dream for me to find my own freedom and the American Dream. She knew I was like my father. Cuba offered no future for me. Although she never said it aloud, she wanted my future to be better than what she had achieved.

She had a different attitude toward me now than toward Yamila. Years before, my half-sister had the opportunity to go to America with her then-boyfriend, Luis, who was thirty years older than she. His mother and brothers were already living in America, and he and Yamila had plans to marry. Mima thought that going to America was a crazy idea.

"What if he dies?" our mother had asked her. "You are in your early twenties. You would be alone in America, without any family." Papa, on the other hand, had encouraged her to go.

Although my father was encouraging ("Don't listen to your family!"), Yamila, being very young, was afraid. She had respect for her stepfather but ultimately listened to her mother and stayed behind and married Luis.

Years passed, and many people left the island. The economy and the Castro regime never changed, but my half-sister and mother had. Now Mima had another daughter ready to escape, and she would not discourage me, even though it was more dangerous now than when Yamila was considering her departure.

Mima gave me her blessing—or "the good-luck kiss," or as we said in Cuba, "Buena suerte"—and then gently pushed me, urging me to leave. She saw the tears welling in my eyes. She looked old and vulnerable, with her gray hair and wrinkled face. I turned and walked away, not looking back, just like Papa told me to do.

I kept my head down until I reached the hospital. I saw Dian waving at me from a green and white Chevrolet. I picked up my pace and jumped into the car, then settled into the backseat. Dian and her son were squeezed in the front seat with the driver. "We are meeting the others at two this afternoon," Dian said.

I kept my head down, hiding my tears. Dian had arranged for this car to take us to Havana City. Emotionally exhausted, I fell asleep.

Dian woke me up. "We are getting close to our destination."

I looked out the window. We had stopped on an isolated road. Dian and I walked on either side of her son, holding his hands. We came upon the man in charge, and he led us to others, gathered in the dark. The remainder of the group was on time.

This venture was so different from the previous time. No sugar plantation lacerating our skin, no canal to cross. The drone of mosquitoes and the smell of swamp water was the same.

I remember the sun saying goodbye, but the mosquitoes did not leave us. They were our constant companions. Every hour some of the men trekked to the ocean, their way lit by a flashlight, to see if the boat was coming. One lookout stayed on the alert for coast guard patrols.

Hours passed. We were left to wait in the dark woods for the boat. The high drone of mosquitoes and the murky stench of swamp water enveloped us. I tried to soothe myself by remembering how many people had made the decision to escape, despite the illegality.

I pushed away thoughts that I was risking my life. I had heard many stories of people who had left Cuba on rafts, in boats, or any makeshift vessels they could piece together to cross those ninety miles to freedom. Some families assumed their loved ones never made it, because they had not heard from them again. They supposed their relatives had drowned or been eaten by sharks. For years in my childhood, that fate was a dark fairy tale we passed among ourselves. Now I was embarking upon that possible horror.

At about three or four in the morning, our boat arrived. As soon as it came into view, we sprang into action. Everyone raced into the ocean and did not let the waist-deep water slow us. I had never been in a boat, and I did not know how to swim. It was too late to worry about that.

I was terrified. No one reached to help anyone else. Each of us was on our own. Dian and I and her son stayed as close to each other as possible, and we helped the boy scramble over the side. As members of the group jumped into the boat, legs and elbows were flying. Dian and I were frantic, afraid the boat would take off with the child and leave us behind.

A man at the back called out, "Slow down. I'll wait for all of you." His voice was strong and authoritative, and I guessed he was the captain. He must have known how desperate we all were, even under the cover of darkness. He was probably more concerned for the soundness of his boat than for us passengers. Dian and I managed to get on board. Then he said, "We are leaving now!"

The vessel took off fast with a roar of an outboard engine, and Dian and I squeezed each other's hand. I prayed that the night would end as soon as possible and that I would soon see land on the horizon.

The next thing I knew, we were surrounded by water in the dark night. Stars shone bright. My heart was beating hard and fast. Leaving behind the coast and the island, I knew that was the last time I would see all that I had left behind. Dian and her son and I held each other tightly. I extricated my right hand and wiggled my fingers inside a plastic bag I had brought with me. It held a picture of Papa and another of San Lazarus.

The small motorboat bounced across the waves, and salty water splashed into my face. I turned and saw the wake in the moonlight. A big man next to the pilot told us that the trip to the keys would take more than two days.

"I thought it would be a couple of hours," someone called out, and that was what I had guessed.

"We must focus on avoiding the coast guard and making it safely to the nearest key in Florida," the big man added. "As long as we touch the land, we will be fine."

Now he went on to explain the "wet foot, dry foot" interpretation of the 1995 revision of the application of the Cuban Adjustment Act of 1966. It says that anyone who emigrated from Cuba and entered the United States would be allowed to pursue residency a year later. That was a goal we all had, but in the near term, all we wanted that night was to see daylight.

In time, I surrendered to the beauty of the sky and the sound of the water and the rhythmic movement of the boat. I sensed how the ocean took us with pleasure and serenity. I felt magic around us. My San Lazarus and Papa were with us. The ecstasy of those first hours did not last.

The men in charge handed out water and drinks. Dian's son was so brave, he was practically a little man. He was quiet and protective of his mother. I had never seen such behavior in a child.

Sometimes the boat accelerated, then it slowed. The vessel was medium size, but I feared it was too small for the eleven passengers and that the back would sink. No one said anything out loud, but we all exchanged fearful glances. We were jammed against each other, shoulder to shoulder. Some squeezed into the corners of the boat, while others sat in the middle like sardines in a can. Dian and I and her son held hands tightly when the waves tossed us up, then dumped us on the other side.

The sun rose and hit us hard. I felt the salt water on my face and the unforgiving sun, and it was like I was on fire. I felt nauseated and threw up several times, as did another woman aboard. No one paid much attention; it was just another occurrence on that severe voyage.

We made an effort to relax. I tried to focus on the bright side, hoping there was one. For a couple of hours, we all shared what we planned to do in America. I said I wanted to be a barber. A couple of weeks before leaving Cuba, I thought cutting hair would be fun. Having short hair in a hot climate made sense, and Florida was hot. I had already taken some classes for becoming a barber. Everyone on board had entrepreneurial ideas, but I was the only barber.

Night fell after a long and trying day. At last we had some relief from the sun, but my face was emanating heat. The darkness awoke our fears. Then the big man in the front made an announcement.

"We might have to leave you all somewhat near a shore. We are running out of gas."

They did what he said. The flashlights came out in the middle of the night, but their beam did not go far. We all peered into the darkness, trying to see land. I did not see any, but the engine idled, and the man yelled, "Everybody out!"

We tumbled over the side of the boat, and I went under the water. My feet could not find the ocean floor. I bobbed up and flailed, my mouth filled with water. I gasped and coughed. Someone grabbed hold of me—I don't know who—and dragged me along with him. I worried about sharks. Soon I felt sand and gained my footing. We all walked fast, determined to get to the shore. It was a marathon, I was so bone tired. I prayed for land and daylight. Only flashlight beams showed the way.

"Mangrove ahead," a man's voice rang out.

Some men were carrying water. Others had big packs on their back. I knew Dian had a small pack for her son's needs. Thinking our trip would take two hours, I had taken only my clear plastic bag with photographs.

The group staggered onto the shoreline. Wherever we were, it was pitch black. This was not civilization, but it had to be a Florida key. We had made it. I lay back on the sand, trying to catch my breath. I guessed we had a few more hours till daylight, but it was an eternity.

I took off my lightweight blue jacket, rolled it up as a wet pillow, and let myself cry. My face felt as if it had come out of an oven, and my body was freezing cold. At last the sun rose. Would anyone see us on this forsaken bit of land and rescue us, or would some travelers eventually find our bleached bones? Hours passed, then more hours.

Each one of us took turns, standing on the edge of the mangrove, searching for a boat. The plan was to scream and wave our arms to attract attention. At around noon, when the scorching sun was high, a small yacht came toward us. They did not get close, but we continued to shout to them for help, even as they disappeared from sight.

We could not afford to spend more days and nights without water. We were all thirsty, and Dian and I were very concerned for her child.

I began to worry about animals that might live in the thick tropical growth behind us.

Shortly before sunset, our lookout ran back to us to say a big boat was coming toward us. We realized it was the United States Coast Guard. Five gun-carrying men came onshore. They looked gigantic to me.

They helped us onto their boat and handed out life jackets and water.

Dian burst into tears, begging them in Spanish not to send us back to Cuba, but the men paid little attention to any of us. We were bedraggled, too tired to sit up straight, and maybe in shock.

Our rescuers took us to shore, where more police were awaiting us. They helped us one by one to disembark and then took us to an office where we were separated for interrogation. An older official with blue

Papa's Cuban drivers licence

eyes sat on a bench across from me. I was shaking from the cold and my fear. He spoke only English, and I did the best I could with sign language and guesswork.

He filled out a form with my name and age and then gestured toward my plastic bag with Papa's picture. "Who is that?" he asked.

"*Mi papa*," I answered.

I looked around the room and saw that the officials were confiscating everything our group had brought with them in their backpacks, including flashlights. With gestures, I told him I needed that picture, and the man left it with me.

After the interviews, we were herded onto a bus. Dian was terrified that her son would be taken from her, and she held tight to his hand. The bus took us to the detention center, and the men were directed to one jail cell, and the women and children to another.

Guards brought us prison clothes, and I was grateful for the dry, baggy pants and blouse and big sandals, all beige. This time our interrogation took hours. "Who brought you to that key?" "Where is the boat now?" So many questions! This time the official was a woman who spoke Spanish.

I can still feel the tension and fear of that interview. I thought I would stay in jail forever, such was their concern for the heavy human trafficking that was (and still is) taking place from Cuba to the Florida Keys. The woman showed me photographs of many men and some of the boats known to be used by the smugglers. She emphasized that I was a victim and not a criminal.

I remained quiet for the whole time. My head was spinning. I still was traumatized by what I had endured, and I was just beginning to comprehend the magnitude of the risk we had taken to escape the dictatorship and find freedom.

She let me go back to my cell, and I cried all the way. I had pent-up tears from fear, uncertainty, pain, and isolation. So many years I had dreamed of this moment. So many promises I had made to myself and to Papa.

We got word that the officials had completed our background checks and were releasing us that very night. Dian and the others called their relatives. I waited beside the boy, then the three of us went outside to wait for Sonia to pick us up. She was most welcoming. I knew this journey with a child would have been difficult for Dian to undertake by herself. I was very happy Alien asked me to come along.

The next day, after a sound sleep, I called my friend Anita, who lived in Miami. She was excited and surprised to hear where I was. She came right over for our happy reunion and invited me to be her houseguest.

⟨ **8** ⟩

English Is Fun

"Nothing and nobody will take me back to Cuba," I vowed to myself. Even though my mother and I were not together, I could not have given her a better gift than being alive, and contacting her was my top priority.

Through Anita I met many Cubans who had recently arrived in the United States. Every day, any given month, people were coming from Cuba, arriving in the keys, with a simple leap of luck. I found a smile of pure joy on the face of every Cuban, to see yet another brother or sister had escaped the Castro regime.

My friends threw a welcome party for me with much food and music and laughter. Anita bought me new clothes and shoes because I had come with nothing. She took me many places, showing me the wonders of Miami.

For my first few weeks, I did not feel as if I was in another place or another country; I felt like I landed on another planet. Back in Cuba, I had heard talk about paradise. Some people in Cuba called Florida *la Otra Orilla*—"The other side." To me, it was paradise. The lights, the traffic, the happiness on every face!

I had dreamed of it for so many years. I looked at the sky and said, "Papa, this is America, the Land of Opportunities. This is the light and the freedom you always yearned for."

I was never much of a city girl. I went to Havana a few times and had always been intrigued by it. How had they built those hotels, I wondered, so big that they could reach the sky? Nevertheless, when I first saw Miami, it was more than a city and more than "little Cuba." It was the paradise that many people described to us still living in Cuba. They acted like they owned it or had just built it.

The true Cuban-Americans, the ones who will never go back to the island, brought with them the fragrance of tobacco, the sugar cane, the Latin music, and the color, and they added spice to the American flavor.

During my first phone call with Mima, I tried to describe the place. I was screaming with excitement, trying to find words for the breathtaking, seductive, and extravagant city.

Mima asked, "How are you doing? Where are you staying?"

I could only reply, "Mima, you have got to see this! So many cars! So big is this city! So clean! And everyone seems to be happy!" The best part was telling her that in only a few days, I had so much clothing and so many shoes from Sonia and Anita.

The places I went downtown were like in the movies, with people playing music on guitars and dancing in the streets. I had seen that in Cuba, but with new eyes, Miami was pure light and magic, like the pictures Papa had painted in words so many times.

After a few weeks of getting my bearings, I began to think about where I was going to live. Anita had her life, and she was married. I did not want to be a burden. I knew I had to find a job, learn the ways of this country, become fluent in the language, save money for a car, and sign up for drivers' education. I did have some driving experience, when

I was twelve and Papa was too drunk to get behind the wheel. That hardly applied now.

My wide-open future began to fall into place when I received a call from my cousin Dania, who lived on Florida's Gulf Coast. She was the daughter of one of my father's brothers. Although Dania was a few years older than I was, we had played together at our grandmother's house on the river.

I remember a birthday celebration when someone hung a piñata, and we cousins struck at it with a stout stick to release candies inside it. Dania asked me to bring her some candy and sent me into the fray while she stayed back. I was the smallest cousin, and when the piñata was breached and candies spilled out, all my cousins piled on top of me in the ensuing chaos. I did not snatch even one sweet.

When I got back on my feet, I saw that Dania was standing on the perimeter, her hands full of candy. On that day I determined that she was strong and smart. Now I felt certain she would be the perfect person for me to stay with as a newcomer to America.

"Come to live with me," Dania said. "I am a single parent, and we can help each other."

My cousin had two children, five-year-old Yunicsky, who was in day care, and eleven-year-old Mario, in middle school. Her husband had recently moved out of the house. He contributed some money to household expenses, but her finances were tight. Dania did not make much as a housekeeper at the Best Western motel in Punta Gorda, almost thirty minutes from her house.

I was excited. She would give me protection and guidance. After a few more weeks in Miami, I called Dania and asked her to pick me up and take me to Florida's West Coast.

"The small town where I have lived for three years is very different from Miami," she warned me. "There is no Latin music."

I realized she was really telling me that the population was not ethnically diverse, and the social life for a single Hispanic person would not have the opportunities of Miami—the dancing and drinking and partying on weekends. Dania was telling me that I would not find many people who spoke Spanish, which might isolate me from making new friends.

None of this discouraged me. I knew already that most Cubans lived in Miami. I intended to learn English as quickly as I could, as Papa had advised. The situation in my new home would motivate me. I would be forced to speak English to get along in my new community. Without mastering the language, I would not be able to get a good job. I would be limited to cleaning jobs, as was the case with Dania.

She and her children spoke Spanish at home, even though her boys were learning English in day care and public middle school.

We were headed across the state to the town of Port Charlotte, an unincorporated community with fewer than fifty-thousand residents in 2009. It was not a fancy place. Almost one-fifth of the residents lived at the poverty level. The next largest town was Punta Gorda. It was situated on the Gulf of Mexico, and the naturally beautiful beaches were unspoiled.

"You might not like Port Charlotte," Dania continued. "If you aren't happy, save some money and go back to Miami."

We arrived at her small concrete ranch house, which was painted light blue. It had two bedrooms. Dania slept in one, and her children shared the other.

She took me to a little room converted from a garage space. It had a twin bed, a closet, and a dresser. In the two weeks I lived in Miami, my friends had given me more clothing than I ever owned in Cuba. I organized my belongings and stuffed the dresser drawers.

As I unpacked, I heard women's voices coming from the kitchen. Someone was saying to my cousin, "I want coffee and a beer."

That person must be Cuban, I thought. Who else would combine hot coffee and a cold beer in the middle of the day? I came out of my room to join them. Dania introduced us, and immediately Yarelis and I became fast friends.

The next day Yarelis helped me find a job by driving me everywhere around town to fill out employment applications. Yarelis helped me often in every way she could.

My first job was as a housekeeper in a hotel. I worked hard all day and studied English at night. On my third day, my supervisor found me in the midst of stripping sheets from a king-sized bed.

"How long have you been cleaning this room?" she asked in English.

I was thrilled. I knew this question from my studies! "I have been here one month," I answered proudly.

The woman's expression screwed up. I could not tell if she was holding back a laugh or a scolding.

Cleaning hotel rooms was the hardest job I ever had, even worse than the tobacco factory when I was sixteen. I had left behind a professional career as a computer educator, and now I was scrubbing toilets. Then I remembered when Mima cleaned houses during the day after Papa died. We had been scrounging for money. Even I cleaned houses and did people's laundry to supplement her meager income. It had not been pleasant, but nothing was worse than what I was doing at the hotel.

Every morning I rode Mario's bicycle to work. On occasion Dania dropped me off at the hotel if it was convenient for her before she took her little boy to daycare. I became single-minded: I needed to save money for my green card—officially known as a Permanent Resident Card—and my purchase of a car.

That plan was dashed when the hotel manager called me into her office after I had worked there for three months. She spoke to me in English, and I did not understand. When she read my face, she said in Spanish, "No mas Trabajo." She handed me my final check. I had been fired.

I cried all the way to Dania's house. Riding the bike, I thought my American Dream was dead. I was humiliated that I had lost my housekeeping job. I was devastated that I could not fulfill Papa's dream.

For weeks I cried at night in my bed. I asked Papa, "Why did you put all these big ideas in me?" I began to compare myself to some people who remained in Cuba, acquaintances who chose to be communists. The system worked for them. Maybe it would have worked for me, too, if Papa had not fed all his discontent and unreachable dreams into my head since I was a child.

"Why did you die and leave me to do this by myself?" Bitter, hot tears fell onto my pillow. "Why did you teach me I could do more and be a success?"

I didn't know English. I lost my job. I had no money. I had moved far from Miami, where everyone speaks Spanish and speaks Cuban and felt like a big Cuban family to me. I could have made it there.

Port Charlotte was smaller and colder and whiter. People stared at me and made fun of me when I spoke my broken English. Their disapproving frowns reminded me of the day long ago in Cuba when I recited that poem, and the school principal called me "crazy" like my father.

I was a nobody. I didn't belong here. I had never belonged anywhere because my father was not a doctor or lawyer or a government employee.

I missed Mima and my bed and our home.

I was unemployed for two months. Dania was already on food stamps, and I, not able to contribute to her household expenses, applied for food stamps as well. I also did what I could to make her life easier, like doing the laundry.

My cousin did laundry on weekends. That a detergent was enhanced with fragrance pleased me. I had never smelled anything like it. In Cuba, Mima and I put two small bars of soap in the washing machine. The clothes smelled clean but could not compare with Dania's clothing.

Dania also had a dryer. In Cuba, we hung our wet garments on a rope on Mima's balcony. They needed a whole day to dry.

My cousin taught me how to use her laundry machine and how to do her housework. Once, I poured bleach into the dispenser where the liquid detergent was supposed to go. I damaged a few pair of slacks and some blouses. I was beside myself, but Dania laughed it off as if she were rich and had no worries. "It's just clothing," she said. "Don't worry about it."

I was so grateful that she did not want me to feel bad. Mostly she stayed in good humor in spite of the pressures on her. Dania had been living in the States for two years, and she was lonesome for her parents, my uncle Tico and his wife, as much as I missed Mima. She rarely had a day off, and we had almost no time to talk. One Sunday when she did,

Dania said, "Let's sit in the living room and watch a videocassette my family just sent to me."

The movie of a family birthday party lit up the television screen. The guests included Mima and Dania's parents and brothers. Uncle Tico reminded me so much of Papa, with the same big, heavy voice, the same face, and the smile as big and pronounced as my father's. Most difficult for me, he was singing, drinking, and laughing like Papa used to do.

Watching the video was ripping my heart out. Seeing my mother on the distant island, not being able to hug her, was unimaginably sad.

I glanced at Dania, and she was crying, too.

"I don't want to watch this anymore," I said quietly, and she turned off the television.

Being older and being a mother, she understood me better than I understood her. She was always trying to protect and care for me, as I knew she would. When Yarelis picked me up in her car to go out dancing almost every Saturday night, Dania did not approve. She feared for my safety at a club at night. At the same time, she wanted me to have a good time. Because I was not yet a mother saddled with the responsibilities of child care, this was my time to dance and experience some of the big world.

Overall I tried very hard not to upset her. When her good nature and sweetness were stretched to the breaking point—usually by her ex-husband or her children—I knew better than to get close to her. And if I was upset with her, I kept my distance. After a day or two of cooling off, she would say, "Let's have a cup of coffee and listen to some music."

That was how we made peace. Our eyes, brimming with tears wanting to drop, would be as clear as a glass of water. We would hold back our tears. We would sit over our coffee and talk about Cuba and the good old days. Sometimes we would eat her recipe for fried pork, which was the best in the world. The next day, life would continue as normal. Still, I knew I had to leave my cousin's house and hospitality. I wanted my own place and an independent life. I wanted a reunion with Mima and a place where we could live together.

I had so many goals, I had to write them down in a journal. I included my most silly, ridiculous secrets. Before closing the cover, I would say, "Thanks for listening to me."

At last I found another housekeeping job. Days, I worked in a nursing home and nights, I cleaned.

At the nursing home, I met a young woman who guided me to the community college. While we were getting to know each other, I had confided that I wanted to earn a college degree, master English, and qualify for a job that paid good money.

The college was relatively close to Dania's house and my workplace. I signed up for English as a Second Language. I was excited that I could work full time and go to college full time. Learning English not only enhanced my chances of finding good jobs, it also altered my ways of thinking about and seeing the world around me. I began to feel more confident and, well, more American. I started to see paradise again.

Red Mustang Convertible

One year had passed since I arrived in America. My Green Card came in the mail, and I was officially a Permanent Resident of the United States. I applied for a Cuban passport to visit Mima, whom I missed terribly. We kept in touch with letters and photographs, but I wanted to be with her.

Every time Mima sent me a photo of herself in front of her house, I could only see the same gray and black pall that I had left behind.

I finally got my Cuban passport, but the Cuban government denied me entry for five years because I had left the island illegally. Since I could not visit her, she would have to visit me.

I became more driven for success. I hunted for job opportunities where I would be obligated to speak English. I found work as a dishwasher in a restaurant where almost all my coworkers were American. The only other Hispanic was a dishwasher.

My employer assigned me to food preparation. I constantly burned my hands on the oven, which was too high for me to reach. I am four feet, nine inches tall, but I top out at five feet, two inches in high heels and on my driver's license. Unfortunately, I could not wear high heels in the kitchen.

I still did not speak the language well, but during this time I could grasp what people said to me in English. The kitchen crew, who earned only eight dollars per hour, did not believe in the American Dream, calling it a "fairy tale." On my break time, I talked to my coworkers in English and shared my goals to finish college and bring Mima to the States. Some of them looked at me as if I were crazy.

I had expected to leave that skepticism behind in Cuba from people fed up with communism. Now I realized that some Americans felt the same way about their own government. They had the same despair in their eyes as Papa had before he died. They were even more defeated than my father. They did not like capitalism, and it did not like them. They blamed the government, the immigration laws, the politicians, and the diversity of religions and races in America. They had more targets for their anger than we had in Cuba. They were disappointed by the people they felt had let them down. Without special skills, education, or the ability to speak proper English, their future was bleak, and they knew it.

For quite some time I was confused or mystified by them. How can people be poor and unhappy in one of the world's richest countries? I did not let their attitude discourage me. I continued to work and practice my English. After two years I found a job in a deluxe department store. I could wear my high heels again! This was momentous.

I continued my transformation into an American. Yes, I missed my Cuban coffee, but I was growing accustomed to Starbucks latte. I missed Mima's rice and beans, but I could cook them at Dania's house. The one thing I could not compensate for was the separation from my mother.

The reality that I could not visit Cuba to see my mother terrified me. What would happen if Mima died, and I could not attend her funeral? I heard many stories from Cubans who came to the States in the 1980s and were not allowed to see their parents back home. Cubans in exile had grown up in a culture where the family bond was like steel. Now they endured the anguish of separation and isolation from their loved ones. I was afraid to go through that heartache.

I was left with only one option: I had to save money and bring Mima to the US. I already had the necessary status of Permanent Resident to start the process. I knew it would take years, however, before my application was approved. It was better to try during these uncertain times than accept defeat before I even started.

Mima pitched in as well. She sold some of her belongings to raise money to pay for a passport and whatever fees would be charged. My sisters wanted to help, but they, too, were struggling financially.

One of my half-sisters was not in favor of the trip. "You are too old," she said to our mother. "What happens if you need medical assistance? Who will take care of you? Not Mory. She is busy with work and college."

Even one of my American college professors gave me her unasked-for advice. "Wait until you graduate. Start your career, and then think about bringing your mother here."

I tried to keep an open mind, but I missed my mother. I wanted her with me, to talk to, to hug and kiss and comfort, and to make up for the time we had lost.

I didn't allow myself to feel too melancholy or too lonely, because I was working full time and carrying a full load of college classes at night or in the morning. Being so busy made the days fly. I concentrated on filling out Mima's paperwork.

Making life easier for me was the old minivan that Dania had given me, so I had my own transportation. A cousin who lived in Tampa drove the two hours south to Port Charlotte for a visit and made me a gift of five hundred dollars so I could afford a license plate. I was so grateful! I hardly knew this relative. She spoke with affection about Papa, as if he were some kind of guru, because his conversations about democracy had inspired her life, too.

"Your father talked at family get-togethers about Cubans who fought and died for the land and freedom, but until I left the island, I didn't fully understand the importance of his words," she said.

My Tampa family felt compassion for me and wanted to help me. They all shared memories about my father, and I told them stories about him that they had not heard. They were also trying to help both Dania and me, two women living together, she being separated from her husband, and I, trying to make it on my own.

After a few months, the minivan's mechanical problems were not worth fixing. I took it to an auto salvage yard where it would be stripped for parts. In exchange I got a little cash, and I applied that to the purchase of a used red Mustang convertible. It was not a classic car like my father's 1957 Ford, but it gave me a sense of freedom. With the top down, I had the wind in my hair and the sun on my shoulders. I blasted Latin music on the radio and looked around at everything. I felt so alive! It was like having Papa next to me.

I remembered the road trips to Grandma's house in my father's Ford. I heard his voice, thick with regret, talking about the American Dream. On those days driving my red sportscar, listening to Orlando Contreras on the radio, I was living not solely for myself; I was living for Papa, too. I was making up for the days when he never found the light or the freedom or even the hope to live another day.

The red Mustang was not just a car. It was a symbol of my dreams and promises to Papa and myself. It stood for the life I wanted and would continue to strive for until I had achieved my goals.

I was obsessed with the American Dream. Every day I met people who wanted the same things I did. I also made contact with many eyes and souls that reminded me of Papa's before he surrendered and died.

I kept learning and opening myself to new experiences. I was exposed to some things that were so unfamiliar, I had no idea what they were, how they were significant, or how they would eventually affect me and help me grow.

When we are born, we must learn everything. I felt like a child, excited and enthusiastic. I knew I was naïve, and I needed to sharpen my best skills to survive and become the "new me." Taken together, they exemplified being "born again in America," as Papa used to say.

At last I had saved enough money to rent my own apartment and move out of Dania's house. I kissed her goodbye but visited her every other day. We drank Cuban coffee and sometimes ate fried pork, rice, and beans.

I felt fully alive in paradise. Everything looked beautiful to me, even the streetlights and neon lights and the cars and the places I went. People were happy . . . or pretended they were. Mima got an appointment at the American embassy and her visa approved. The last phase of waiting had begun. Soon, I hoped, she would have her visa in her hand.

On a rare Sunday off from work, I went to the beach, sat on the sand, and enjoyed the view. A man jogged by with his black Lab running at his side. The dog came over to me, and his owner followed. *"Hola,"* he said. *"Hablo poquito Español?"*

He was an American with some Hispanic ancestors. We found common ground, and just like that, I had a new American friend. I spoke English with him, and after a few sentences, he said, "I love your accent."

I began to think I spoke perfect English but with an accent. Some people, especially men, commented on my accent in a positive way. Others dismissed me as just another immigrant. The first time someone treated me as "less than," I took on the responsibility of embracing America. Papa had never learned to embrace Cuba and felt like he was in enemy territory. Now, not only did I want to speak English well, I wanted to understand the American culture and become a part of it.

My new friend was a huge help with that. He taught me to appreciate rock and roll, and I introduced him to Cuban coffee, which he fell in love with.

I thought about how I would teach my mother when she came to join me in America, even though I myself still had so much to learn. Finally, after five long years of waiting, she had her visa, and I made her plane reservations. She would fly into Miami on January 25, my father's birthday.

I left Port Charlotte early in the morning for Mima's noontime arrival. Yeralis offered to ride with me. This would be my first time at the Miami Airport, and I needed help with everything. My friend Sonia and her husband, Alien, arranged to meet me in a cafeteria in the town of Hialeah, near the airport, and give me a hand. After having a cup of coffee, Yeralis and I followed their car to the airport and into short-term parking, then we walked together to the waiting area for arrivals.

I was nervous and happy. They were delighted for me that Mima and I would be together again at last.

I focused my gaze on the big door separating the gates and the terminal. Many passengers came through, and I looked behind them for my mother. I saw her from a distance, and like a little child after the first day of school, I ran into her open arms. We hugged each other, and she embraced me strongly, like never before. Happy tears danced down my cheeks, and I did not bother to brush them away.

Mima was crying as well. On the day I left Cuba all those years ago, my mother pushed me away on my shoulder, urging me to go. Now she made sure I stayed by her side. She did not release my hand.

I sneaked some glances at her. She was older and smaller. She looked so different. I knew she was Mima, but pronounced lines etched her face and under her eyes. Those wrinkles were so strong and vivid, I could read them, like words on the page of a book. Each one defined her tears and regrets. Every one showed a night spent not in sleep but in prayer to God or any saint that might protect my well-being in the States. Every wrinkle told of loneliness and uncertain thought. Every one under her eyes reflected the love of a mother for a beloved child far away.

The years of separation forced both of us to grow because we had lost something important.

As we walked to the car, we held hands, inseparable. No one could have pulled us apart.

For the first days, we talked nonstop, sharing memories to catch each other up with our lives during our separation. I felt as if we had lost those years, but now I was getting them back, filling the hole in my heart. Mima moved in with me, just like old times.

She was in her late sixties, though, and I came to realize that it was too late for her to understand the American Dream or achieve it for herself.

I left every morning for work, and I went to school at night. She found it difficult to be alone so much. She struggled to understand my new American friends when they came to visit us. She could not make sense of their words or their facial expressions.

After a few months, Mima began to miss her other daughters in Cuba, and her grandchildren. Yamila's much-older husband passed away at seventy-three, and now she was a widow raising twin teenagers. Mima knew Yamila needed her help and support.

I was crushed thinking of saying goodbye to my mother, but I understood that not all of us came to America to be born again. Some Cuban immigrants never felt as if they belonged here, even if they enjoyed a better life than under communism. Some Cubans died in America, filled with regret, just as Papa had died in despair in Cuba. The only difference was that they lived on a different coast.

I came to understand better why Papa never tore himself away from Cuba. He grew up with loving parents and brothers and sisters. Their bonds never loosened as they got older and had families of their own. He could not say goodbye to those family concerts at Grandma and Grandpa's house on the river. The Caballos were never famous on television or YouTube, Instagram, or Twitter. That made no difference.

My grandparents had eleven children, and their upbringing nurtured love for each other! Unlike other families I knew, the Caballos kept family dramas to themselves and at a minimum. They enjoyed every birthday together and supported one another at every funeral. All members of the youngest generation still expressed the full extent of the Carballo family's love at reunions.

In this remarkable family, Papa held a place of honor. He was universally loved by his brothers and sisters and their spouses. He was famous for his mother and father and for his brothers and sisters, whom the community held in high regard. How could he leave them for America? He could not. That esteem was the one thing he could not buy in the United States.

My half-sisters loved and respected him, even though he was not a blood relative. Manuel, his son, adored him, even though for many practical reasons, Papa could not raise him. If I knew Papa, that was probably one of his biggest regrets—not being able to raise his only son.

Throughout my childhood, though, he made sure Manuel was as much a part of his life as I was.

Now, seeing how Mima had changed during our separation, I understood Papa's choices better. He watched his parents grow old and die. He never learned to prosper under the dictatorial system, did not get a new car or provide us with a better house. He let moonshine kill him slowly. But he celebrated his siblings' every joy and was laid to rest next to the people who loved him the most. He lived on in the fond memories of the survivors.

Mima did not belong with me, but she was living a gift of experience that Papa never had. After a few months she returned to Cuba and into the arms of family and friends. Ever since, she continued to travel back and forth. With her comes the black and gray pall, but when she goes home, she takes with her a rainbow of every color and bags filled with stories and promises to share with everyone living on the island.

⟨ **10** ⟩

Becoming

After Mima left, I kept myself busy trying to finish my college degree and working a fulltime job. One day at work, a voice that stopped me and caused me to turn around said, "Hello."

His black eyes and the intensity of his gaze startled me. I thought I knew him from somewhere—maybe in my dreams. His expression held love and romance. I knew he was ready for both. He looked attractive in a black T-shirt with bright-green details.

I approached him. We exchanged a few words. I liked what he said. Javier and I began to see each other at work and then at my house. Then Spanish blood began to control us and our romance.

In Cuba a saying goes, "You fall in love only once." Falling in love was, for me, more terrifying than the nights I sat on a small boat making for America. I knew how cold the heart feels when we lose someone we love. I remembered the chills in my heart when my husband betrayed me . . . when I lost my best friend . . . when I buried my father . . . when Mima went back home. Even leaving the land where I was born and raised—the smell of tobacco, the taste of moonshine—taught me to avoid that kind of pain again. I wanted my carefree, unattached life of driving my convertible, drinking my Starbucks, and enjoying the breeze in my hair and the air on my face while I blasted Latin music on the radio. I was afraid that if I fell in love again, I would lose all the freedom I had risked so much for to have in my life.

I did not need a man to help or protect me. That had been necessary in Cuba, but not in the United States. When I was living on the island, most of the women were single or divorced, like my half-sisters, with more than two children they were raising on their own. The women I grew up with were disappointed with their existence and sad all the time. As for the children, they were no better off. They cried day and night and grew up unhappy. Those were my memories, not what I supposed was true.

I battled with my heart. I tried to discourage him, giving Javier all my reasons why we didn't need to fall in love. On the other hand, without realizing it, I had lost direction in my life. No longer did I have the roadmap that comes from having a goal. No longer did I yearn to get to America; I was already there.

A few months passed, and the heat of our crazy Hispanic romance had cooled enough to allow for clearer thinking. We were still together. We made promises that we kept. I wanted children; he did not have any yet. I was in my early thirties, and Javier was in his mid-forties. After much discussion, we decided to have a baby.

At the perfect time in our life together, we welcomed a healthy, beautiful baby girl into this world and named her Savanna. I was breastfeeding and returned to school to earn enough credits to complete my Associates degree. Under normal circumstances, a student needs two years to complete the program, but that time had come and gone.

I adored my daughter, but I fought against the new woman I had become—a stay-at-home mom. I missed the girl in the convertible who had big dreams. I had no freedom and was angry at myself most of the time.

Javier rented a new home so the three of us could live together. Then my mother came for a visit, stayed with us for quite some time, and inserted herself into the middle of my personal life. Javier wanted just our intimate little family of three in the house, and he missed our privacy when Mima was around.

My mother was a product of our Cuban culture, where family members are so close. She wanted to be involved in everything, like when it had been just the two of us. And Mima was very emotional. Javier was from Ecuador, a democracy in South America. Its culture differed from Cuba's, and besides that, he had a quiet personality.

The situation was terrible for me. My loyalties were torn, and I did not want to hurt either of them.

Occasionally Mima returned to Cuba to visit my half-sisters and her grandchildren. She still had a small apartment there, and I tried to convince her to sell the apartment and give me the proceeds to buy her a house in the States. She never did. As I look back, I realize it was the best decision she ever made, because she was already thinking of staying permanently on the island. I would have regretted her losing her small home there.

Despite the friction between Javier and Mima, I cried at night, thinking of my mother going back to Cuba and my not seeing her frequently. I had to remind myself that I couldn't have it both ways, and now I had a new family with my first loyalty to my husband.

Being a new mother gave me more understanding of Mima as a woman and a mother. I was in awe that she raised four girls and grandchildren in a communist country, with no education and no money most of the time. She was a hero, but I had never understood that before now. Mima's journey had not ended yet, and she faced every challenge with great courage and heart.

When Savanna was eighteen months old, I was expecting our second child. Javier and I were very happy. We hosted a gender-reveal party at our home with pink confetti inside a black balloon. We popped it together, and our friends and relatives cheered. Savanna didn't understand what was going on, but she shrieked with delight. Daddy wanted a boy, but he adored Savanna, so he was excited about having another daughter.

I didn't care about the gender, as long as our baby would be healthy like Savanna. I envisioned my blue eyes and my wide smile on our infant's face. I was already thinking about a perfect Christmas photo with our family of four.

I was still in college with one more course credit in math to complete before earning my Associates degree in Art. My class in Developmental Algebra focused on creating a strong foundation in that discipline. I had almost achieved my goal, but it wasn't easy because of the nausea accompanying my condition. One morning I had to stop more than once on my way to school to empty my stomach.

I had a final exam that day, and I was nauseated and dizzy and tense. I had to pass algebra, complete an elective course, and then I would be done with this phase of school.

I did miserably on the exam, and I did not pass the final. I was frustrated and disappointed in myself. How would I redo algebra when I would have a toddler and an infant to take care of? It seemed I would have to put off my dreams for a while.

A few weeks passed, and I had an ultrasound of my belly. I came home to find a voicemail from my doctor asking me to come into her office. She sounded so serious, I asked Javier to come with me. We brought Savanna, and Javier's mother came, too, to watch our daughter.

I filled out forms for twenty minutes, and then a radiology technician brought us inside the exam room. She showed us the ultrasound on a light screen.

"Something is wrong," I thought. In my first pregnancy, I had a few fibroids in my uterus, but they didn't interfere with a healthy pregnancy or our baby, so I was not fearful. The technician excused herself, and my obstetrician entered. She was not her usual pleasant, upbeat self. In a professional, sad voice she said, "Your baby girl has a birth defect—a cleft palate and lip."

I was shocked. Until that day I thought birth defects occurred only in poor countries. If I were still in Cuba, then maybe I could understand why that had happened, but not here!

Javier was calm. He said nothing. I don't know how he was able to hide his emotions. I knew he would be as affected as I was. I cried, though, and did not know what to say or do.

We left the exam room and joined my mother-in-law and Savanna in the anteroom. "How is the baby?" Javier's mother asked.

"Everything is good," he told her, not wanting to upset her.

On our way home, we stopped at a restaurant. I hid the terrible pain in my heart. When we got home, my mother-in-law went on her way, and I could cry my heart out. This pain was all over my body, a kind of anguish I never wanted to suffer. I could feel the mark on my baby's face. I could see it in my imagination.

"Maybe there is some mistake…?" Javier suggested. "Something wrong with the technology of the ultrasound? Maybe it's just a mark on the face of our little one, and it will disappear. Everything is probably just the same as they were with Savanna."

To be certain, we made an appointment in Tampa, at St. Joseph's Children's Hospital. It was a two-hour drive from our house.

The doctors and nurses there explained our baby's situation with many details beyond my comprehension. I knew that if I had this baby, she would be bullied her entire life. How would I teach a beloved child to understand and endure the suffering, when I was still learning it myself?

As hard as it was for both Javier and me, I decided to have an abortion. I went inside the clinic myself, and he would pick me up in two hours.

I lay down on the gurney and asked the nurse if I could listen to music through my headphones, and she said yes. I played my father's favorite song by Orlando Contreras and turned up the volume. I knew on that day, I was not alone; Papa was there with me, holding my hand, assuring me everything was fine.

Over the previous two weeks, Javier and I had talked and talked about what to do. Now, as he drove me home, we were silent. I felt empty.

For a few days many feelings shook me that only I could understand. They were shame and regret.

Again Papa came to my rescue. "You are born again," he reminded, "having the opportunity for a new beginning."

At that moment I understood the broad sweep of my father's doctrine from the time I was a girl. "Born again" applied not only to coming to America. It implied a courage and optimism to keep going every time life took me down. As long as I was able to get up off the floor, I had another chance to begin again. My father's last look helped me to hold my head up and feel confident of the future, and laugh.

Papa taught me how to live, not die, even when I was dying.

Freedom Is within Us

Every night when I went to sleep, fear and doubt climbed into bed next to me. They reminded me how many times I had failed some college classes and how insurmountable were the challenges for me to graduate.

After much battling with myself, now I was taking my final class. I needed the three credits to complete the required sixty hours for a General Associate of Art degree. Instead of the standard two years, I had needed thirteen.

The college administrative offices sent me an invitation to my graduation ceremony on December 10, 2021, at the Bradenton (Florida) City Convention Center, at six-fifty PM. The college allotted me four tickets for myself, Javier, Savanna, and Mima. I bought my cap, gown, and tassel.

Despite all evidence to the contrary, my thoughts nagged me: You are not going to graduate this year. . . . You will get an email saying the college has made a mistake.

I had good reason for jangled nerves. The prior semester, after completing the two three-credit algebra course requirements for graduation, the college notified me I was still short one math credit. This was devastating. I had already failed math more than once.

I did not have the luxury of time. I was home-schooling Savanna, I had a busy schedule at home, and I was helping with my husband's business. I could not believe the school was requiring yet another math course. I had no time to go to campus and sit in a classroom several nights a week, let alone devote hours to studying and completing home-work assignments.

The injustice made me question my goal. Maybe I had done enough. I took myself back to those days when I petitioned San Lazarus. My heart was hungry for a deeper spiritual connection. For years my sister, Javier, and some of my Christian friends had been talking to me about Jesus. They encouraged me to be born again in Christ. Because I grew up in a communist country, their discussions included terms and concepts that were unfamiliar to me and therefore difficult to understand.

Even so, I found myself bowing before God. Just like when I was a teen-ager, I petitioned God for help. I spoke to him like when I was a little girl.

That night I wrote a poem. Unlike my father's poem, mine was not about communism. I was talking to the night, to the stars and the moon and Papa, and to God above all.

Your dark blanket sparkles
And comforts me
When I look up.
Some nights I just look up
To find joy in your dark blanket.

Your dark blanket never leaves me.
Sometimes it is your dark blanket and me,

And I ask myself,
"Did someone steal your light?"

Then the next night comes.
Is it your dark blanket and me again?
I look up, there you are again.
Your dark blanket never leaves me.

Finally your dark blanket shows me some light.
This time you bring some company.
On your dark blanket,
The moon, the constellations, the stars.
Then sometimes,
Only sometimes,
I don't fear the day.
I cover myself with your dark blanket,
And you place some sparkles on me.

Before I fell asleep, I whispered, "God, allow me to walk to the podium to receive my diploma!"

And he did.

My saving grace came in the form of an online math class. Remote learning was fairly new, but the Covid-19 pandemic made it a necessity. Now I could take care of my daughter, help with the administrative tasks in Javier's expanding business, keep up with my household responsibilities, and fulfill my math requirements without going to campus.

Finally Graduation Day arrived. I woke up early and checked my email for notices from my college to say I had not graduated. I found nothing in my In Box but still felt unsure. I called the administration office. What if I had not passed the math class I completed online? Would the dean not call my name during the ceremony?

The woman who answered my call suggested I relax. "I will see you at the ceremony," she assured me. Then she added, "In the worst-case scenario, you can always retake the class if you did not get a passing grade."

Being invited to graduation was no guarantee that I had enough math credits now. She said, "You are invited because that was your last course."

I bombarded myself with doubt and fear. I wanted this moment so badly. Over and over I had visualized myself walking across the stage to accept my diploma. I even pictured myself standing at the podium, reciting my poem in front of the student body, like Papa had taught me.

All I wanted, all I ever wanted as my ultimate goal, was to make my father proud. I wanted to let him know that all his lessons about the American Dream had changed my life for the better. In the process, I learned about coping with failures and doubts as much as I did about pushing forward for success.

The morning of graduation, my mother was at home with us, making a fourth pot of coffee. She knew I was nervous, and she tried to hide her own concern. Staying busy was always a good strategy, so I went to my bedroom to do my hair. Javier was there getting ready. I needed to get Savanna dressed.

Bradenton's auditorium was approximately an hour from our house. We left early in case we ran into heavy traffic. That turned out to be the case; an accident ahead slowed our progress. Javier remained calm while I fretted we might be late. I made every attempt to calm myself.

At last we arrived. Javier dropped me at the entrance, where a woman sat behind a table, checking people in and handing them seat assignments. Mima and Savanna stayed with Javier to park the car in the vast lot.

At the front of the queue, I introduced myself to the woman. She scrolled down the list of graduates' names, then looked up at me. "Congratulations," she said with a warm smile and handed me my admission ticket.

My nerves faded. Inside the auditorium, I looked around in awe at the other graduates. I was not the only one in astonishment. For two years, because of Covid-19, ceremonies had been canceled, and students' certificates arrived in the mail. Some ceremonies took place in parking lots with graduates in face masks maintaining social distance. Other graduations took place on Zoom. For me to achieve the culmination of my struggles and hard work, I wanted to walk across a stage. For me, there would be emotion in that moment beyond my comprehension.

My fellow graduates were of diverse ages and ethnicities. I belonged in this group. I did not see myself as older. I did not care about my student loan debts, my nationality, or my accent. We all had our doubts but also our own dreams and goals. The atmosphere in the room was alive with optimism, ambition, and perseverance.

I saw many women holding their child's hand or their husband pushing an infant in a stroller. I was amazed by how many men and women had chosen to complete this journey.

I wanted to take photographs but realized I had left my phone in the car. Oh, no!

Over the PA system I heard, "Moraima Carballo, your father is waiting for you outside."

The announcement jolted me, but I knew it was Javier, and he had brought me my cell phone. Walking back to the auditorium, I laughed under my breath. "Thank you, God, for my father's wink from heaven." He was saying, "I am proud of you." Indeed, when I walked inside, my husband sent me a text message saying: "I am sure your papa would be proud of you. God bless you."

The graduates were filing in to take our seats at the front. Behind us were the staff members. To our left and right were relatives and friends chanting and applauding. I looked around, trying to locate my family. I couldn't find them. Then I heard a whistle from my right side. I recognized it as Javier's. I found them to my right, with my husband pointing me out to Mima and Savanna.

Looking at him now was one of my life's greatest joys since meeting him. I was not just making my father proud. My husband was seeing the mother of his child, his friend and wife, as someone who will take on every challenge to accomplish a goal.

Five-year-old Savanna didn't understand the significance of the occasion beyond seeing that Mommy was happy, which made her happy, too. When she was older, having a mother with a college degree would make a difference and might inspire her to higher education and a better life.

Tears of joy ran down Mima's cheeks.

Every time the dean read a name from the podium, my heart beat faster.

"Moraima Carballo!" came my name from the podium.

I walked across the stage like any other young American, feeling the dream and ambition in the moment. I heard my husband and daughter chanting my name.

"Mommy! Go, Mommy!" Savanna called out.

I had the honor of standing next to Carol F. Probstfeld, Doctor of Education and president of the State College of Florida. As she handed me my certificate and her congratulations, a photographer took our picture.

I held my diploma like a new mother cradles her precious infant. Tears of happiness smudged my mascara. I didn't care. I took a deep breath of freedom—freedom of choice, the options opened to me by a higher education. Even though I thought I had been born free, I had not known until now what real freedom was. A true understanding came to me in the midst of those thousands of people in that room—students, professors, parents, and children.

I saw that freedom had always been with me. I had been fighting, looking for it, then ultimately found it in my blood and in my roots. Indeed, freedom is in the heart.

Epilogue

Former president Jimmy Carter was correct when he wrote in his book *Faith: A Journey for All* (Simon & Schuster, 2019): "We must welcome changing times, but cling to principles that never change."

He continued, "I would say that 'cling to' meant 'have faith.'"

When Carter was president, Papa used to talk about him with positive feelings. "He cares for humans in general," he said. "Not just as the president but as a human being."

I purchased the Nobel Prize winning book after I saw an interview with him on television. It reminded me of Papa talking about democracy and freedom. It is a great book.

Nowadays, I could not understand my father's doctrine about the American Dream any better. If it were not for my faith, how could we talk about any dream? My journey took years. I changed and suffered some pain and loss. Unforgettable people appeared and helped me along my way.

Life is a magical ride. We can only take the leap if we have faith.

When I met my husband, he made many promises that included my American Dream. I created a vision board that I hung on my wall at home. It included the college, a house, a convertible automobile, and most of all, a family of my own.

I have been fortunate enough to enjoy a family in my own home and a college degree.

For the last seven years, I have been caring for my daughter as a stay-at-home mom. I have awarded myself the title of CEO of our household.

I have also helped my husband in his commercial cleaning and construction business and learned with him how to be an entrepreneur.

On the other hand, being separated from my Cuban family is a challenge. Yamila and Xiomara are my "half-sisters," but that sounds more distant than we actually are.

The twins from Yamila's side, Marina Felicia Valdez and Ramon Miguel Valdez, are still in Cuba and studying medicine. In two more years, they will be the first doctors in our family. I have not seen them for thirteen years, and I hope one day I can see them as well as my other nephews and cousins.

Some years ago, my older half-sister Yuly had the opportunity to come to the States with her husband and their three sons. They are living in West Palm Beach, FL. Spending holidays with them makes me happy. I wish we lived close enough to enjoy a cup of coffee together, but we are a two-hour drive apart.

My cousin Dania moved to Miami. She travels often to Cuba and sends me photographs of our grandparents' house and the river in their backyard. She now has her degree as a registered nurse and has achieved her own American Dream.

Mima is still struggling to cope with that dream. For her on some occasions, it is a nightmare. She is bouncing from my house in Port Charlotte to Yuly's house on the east side of the state, to Cuba to visit her other daughters and grandchildren.

Savanna is learning Spanish so she and Mima can converse, and my daughter is also teaching Mima some basic English. I can hear them laughing and playing together during Mima's visits. Savanna loves to teach and have fun, just like me.

Have I achieved the American Dream? Some time ago I was relaxing with my husband on the patio behind our home. He and I decorated it with a colorful hammock, chairs, and an old bicycle as an accessory. We lounged in the shade of two leafy trees we had planted. A breeze carried the song of birds. Our daughter splashed in a kiddie pool, and droplets on water sparkled on her face as she sang a song Mima had taught her.

I am living the American Dream, I thought at that moment, sighing with contentment.

But that was not the ending. Now you are turning the pages of this book, which is another dream come true.

My father's dream was not specific to him and me nor to Cuba. All around the world are countries where poverty, discrimination, and dictatorships do not allow their people to dream big.

Only in America can someone like me believe that I can write words on a paper and reach the world and inspire others to do so.

Moraima Carballo
Port Charlotte, Florida
April 4, 2022

Author's Note

For the past seven years as a stay-at-home mom, I was able to bring this book alive. From time to time I felt the necessity to share the events that transformed my life from the beginning of my childhood in Cuba until now, here in America.

This book begins with two wonderful humans, The Dreamer and The Realist. One taught me that nothing was beyond my reach and that life was better for those who laugh and love unconditionally. The Dreamer taught me to work hard and not stop, because after achieving one goal, the next one is on its way. The Realist was my favorite for teaching me that not every dream comes true. Some dreams die along the way. Understanding that made me persistent.

Having lived under communism until I was twenty-seven, escaping the island in the middle of the night, and coming to America in a small boat with strangers was a daring, daunting experience. I found my own path in the new world of America. I chased goal after goal: learning to speak and write in English; getting a driver's license; supporting myself financially; and earning a college degree in Art. I fell in love and married, and we have a beautiful young daughter. We own a successful business and a lovely home.

Having gained enough knowledge of the English language, I decided to share my story with you. My confidence is still growing with the help of others: college professors, family, friends, and special help from my husband and my editor, Laurie Rosin. When I told Laurie that I did not feel confident as a writer or grammarian, she replied, "You put this story together, and it is a work of art." That gave me more confidence, coming from someone who has been a successful editor for forty-three years. Now she has become a friend.

As a stay-at-home mother residing in the United States for thirteen years, I find myself believing in real-life fairy tales. As a child, my concept of the American dream was "a fairy tale." I thought only immigrants hungered for success. Obviously that concept is too limiting. Whoever you are, wherever you were born and call "home," the American dream is real and worth pursuing.

While this book opens with those two characters—The Realist and The Dreamer—it does not end with them. It continues with you, inspired to see the endless possibilities for a better tomorrow.

About the Author

Moraima Carballo, an émigré from Cuba, earned an Associate of Art degree from the State College of Florida, Manatee-Sarasota campus. For the past seven years, she has been the office manager for a commercial cleaning and construction business founded by her husband and home-schooled their six-year-old daughter. Her love of family and their encouragement gave her the strength to pursue her writing projects.

Look for Moraima's exciting new book in 2024, *It Was the Mirror.*